D1288658

LAUGH YOUR SOCKS OFF!

WORLD'S
BEST
(AND WORST)
KNOCK-
KNOCK
JOKES

GEORGIA BETH

Lerner Publications • Minneapolis

**Knock, knock. Who's there?
Hee.
Hee who?
Hee who ha-ha. Gotcha, tee-hee!**

Lerner Publications Company
A division of Lerner Publishing Group, Inc.
241 First Avenue North
Minneapolis, MN 55401 USA

For reading levels and more information, look up this title at www.lernerbooks.com.

Main body text set in Billy Infant Regular.
Typeface provided by SparkyType.

Library of Congress Cataloging-in-Publication Data

Names: Beth, Georgia, editor.
Title: World's best (and worst) knock-knock jokes / [edited] by Georgia Beth.
Description: Minneapolis : Lerner Publications, 2017. | Series: Laugh your socks off!
Identifiers: LCCN 2017010172 (print) | LCCN 2017027379 (ebook) | ISBN 9781512483567 (eb pdf) |
    ISBN 9781512483482 (lb : alk. paper)
Subjects: LCSH: Knock-knock jokes—Juvenile literature. | Wit and humor, Juvenile.
Classification: LCC PN6231.K55 (print) | LCC PN6231.K55 W67 2017 (ebook) | DDC 818/.60208—dc23

LC record available at https://lccn.loc.gov/2017010172

Manufactured in the United States of America
4-51365-33166-7/8/2021

Knock, knock. Who's there?
T. rex
T. rex who?
Tyrannosaurus rex. Run!!!

Knock, knock. Who's there?
Snore
Snore who?
Dinosnore!

Knock, knock. Who's there?
The two-headed dinosaur
The two-headed dinosaur who?
Hello! Hello!

Knock, knock. Who's there?
Rap
Rap who?
V to the E to the L to the O
to the C to the I to the R to the A
to the P to the T to the O to the R!

Knock, knock. Who's there?
Goat
Goat who?
Goat to the door to see who's knocking!

Knock, knock. Who's there?
Alpaca
Alpaca who?
Alpaca bag for our trip!

HA!
HA!

4

Knock, knock. Who's there?
Otto
Otto who?
Otto be careful in the shark tank.

Knock, knock. Who's there?
Noah
Noah who?
Noah any kittens that need a good home?

5

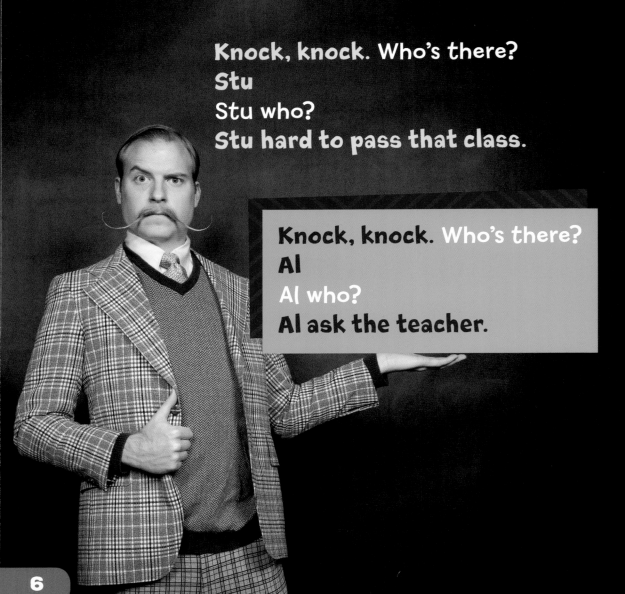

Knock, knock. Who's there?
Shirley
Shirley who?
Shirley you studied for the test.

Knock, knock. Who's there?
Stu
Stu who?
Stu hard to pass that class.

Knock, knock. Who's there?
Al
Al who?
Al ask the teacher.

Knock, knock. Who's there?
Keith
Keith who?
Keith practicing your spelling.

Knock, knock. Who's there?
Stan
Stan who?
We should Stan for the
Pledge of
Allegiance.

KNEE-SLAPPER

Knock, knock. Who's there?
Broken pencil
Broken pencil who?
Never mind. It's pointless.

Knock, knock. Who's there?
Harriet
Harriet who?
Harriet up. The library closes soon!

Knock, knock. Who's there?
Will
Will who?
Will you help me find a book?

Knock, knock. Who's there?
Avery
Avery who?
Avery book in the series is awesome.

>>>>>>>>>>>>>>>>>>>>>>>>

Knock, knock. Who's there?
Brie
Brie who?
Brie sure to return your books on time.

GROANER AWARD

Knock, knock. Who's there?
Emma
Emma who?
Emma wrong, or is this book hilarious?

Knock, knock. Who's there?
Gus
Gus who?
Gus who struck out?

>>>>>>>>>>>>>>>>>>>>>>>>>

Knock, knock. Who's there?
Anita
Anita who?
Anita new hockey stick. Mine broke!

Knock, knock. Who's there?
Hugo
Hugo who?
Hugo long, and I'll
pass it to you.

Knock, knock. Who's there?
Courtney
Courtney who?
She's a beast out on the Court-ney.

Knock, knock. Who's there?
Paul
Paul who?
Bet you can't do ten Paul-ups!

Knock, knock. Who's there?
Ken
Ken who?
Ken you tell I like glitter?

Knock, knock. Who's there?
Alma
Alma who?
ALMA CRAYONS ARE MISSING!

Knock, knock. Who's there?
Sid
Sid who?
Won't you Sid down for your portrait?

Knock, knock. Who's there?
Harold
Harold who?
Harold is this painting?
It looks ancient.

Knock, knock. Who's there?
Harmony
Harmony who?
Harmony stars are there in the sky?

Knock, knock. Who's there?
Ash
Ash who?

ASH-TRONAUT TO THE RESCUE!

Knock, knock. Who's there?
Juno
Juno who?
Juno the moon isn't
made of cheese, right?

Knock, knock. Who's there?
Flo
Flo who?
Help—I'm Flo-ating away!

HA! HA!

KNEE-SLAPPER

Knock, knock. Who's there?
The interrupting alien!
The interrupt—
Blee bloop bleeee!

Knock, knock. Who's there?
Trick
Trick who?
Trick or treat!

Knock, knock. Who's there?
Iris
Iris who?
Iris it was
Thanksgiving
every day.

HA! HA!

16

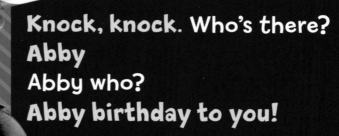

Knock, knock. Who's there?
Abby
Abby who?
Abby birthday to you!

Knock, knock. Who's there?
Noah
Noah who?
Noah-body. April Fool's!

GROANER AWARD

Knock, knock. Who's there?
Warren
Warren who?
Warren any green today?
It's Saint Patrick's Day!

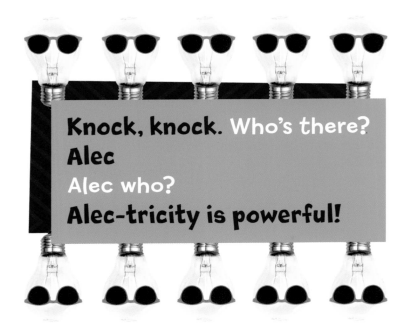

Knock, knock. Who's there?
Alec
Alec who?
Alec-tricity is powerful!

Knock, knock. Who's there?
Ya
Ya who?
Yahoo! I love science!

>>>>>>>>>>>>>>>>>>>>>>>>>

Knock, knock. Who's there?
Chemicals
Chemicals who?
Don't overreact.

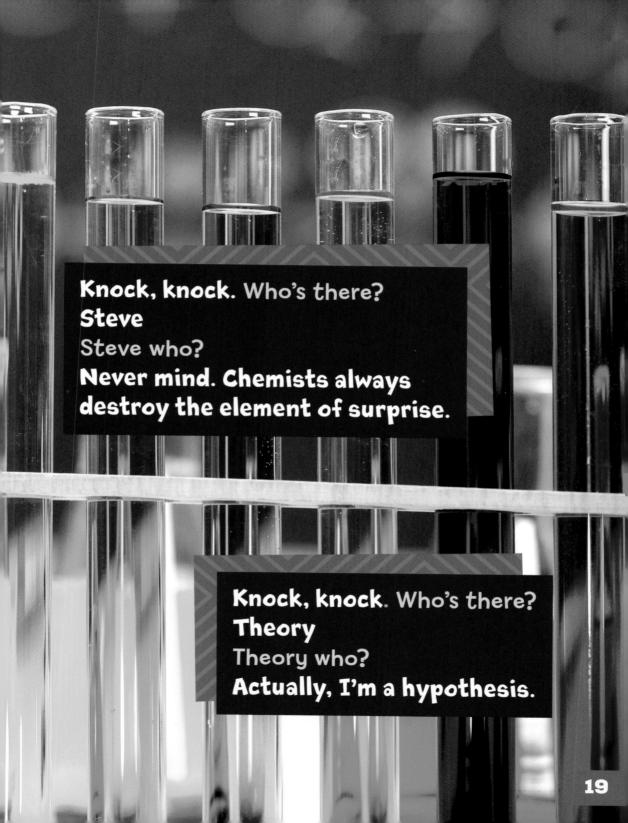

Knock, knock. Who's there?
Steve
Steve who?
Never mind. Chemists always destroy the element of surprise.

Knock, knock. Who's there?
Theory
Theory who?
Actually, I'm a hypothesis.

Knock, knock. Who's there?
Dee
Dee who?
Dee-licious!

Knock, knock. Who's there?
Justin
Justin who?
You're Justin time for spaghetti.

Knock, knock. Who's there?
Ice cream
Ice cream who?
Ice cream right now if you don't open that door!

Knock, knock. Who's there?
General Lee
General Lee who?
Generally, I like hot dogs
better than hamburgers.

>>>>>>>>>>>>>>>>>>>>>>>>>

Knock, knock. Who's there?
Alex
Alex who?
Alex if you can stay for dinner.

>>>>>>>>>>>>>>>>>>>>>>>>>

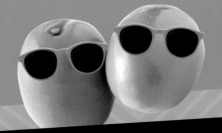

Knock, knock. Who's there?
Lettuce
Lettuce who?
Lettuce in already!

GROANER AWARD

Knock, knock. Who's there?
Olive
Olive who?
Olive you.

Knock, knock.
Who's there?
Hip
Hip who?
No, hip-hop!

Knock, knock. Who's there?
Moo
Moo who?

THE COWBELL MOO-SICIAN!

Knock, knock. Who's there?
Sing
Sing who?
Wholalalalaaaa!

Knock, knock.
Who's there?
Turnip
Turnip who?
Turnip the beet!

KNEE-SLAPPER

Knock, knock. Who's there?
Yodel lay he
Yodel lay he who?
I didn't know you could yodel!

Knock, knock. Who's there?
Wooden shoe
Wooden shoe who?
Wooden shoe like to hear another joke?